ABSENT HERE

PITT POETRY SERIES

Terrance Hayes
Nancy Krygowski
Jeffrey McDaniel

Editors

ABSENT HERE

BRET SHEPARD

University of Pittsburgh Press

This book is the winner of the 2023 Donald Hall Prize for Poetry, awarded by the Association of Writers and Writing Programs (AWP). AWP, a national organization serving more than three hundred colleges and universities, has its headquarters at George Mason University, Mail Stop 1E3, Fairfax, VA 22030.

The Donald Hall Prize for Poetry is made possible by the generous support of Amazon.com.

Published by the University of Pittsburgh Press, Pittsburgh, Pa., 15260
Copyright © 2024, Bret Shepard
All rights reserved
Manufactured in the United States of America
Printed on acid-free paper
10 9 8 7 6 5 4 3 2 1

ISBN 13: 978-0-8229-6728-6
ISBN 10: 0-8229-6728-6

Cover art: Sonny Mauricio on Unsplash
Cover design: Melissa Dias-Mandoly

For Weston

For Boden

CONTENTS

Bedtime Story with Eagle and Sun   xiii

I.

Here but Elsewhere   3

Radiation Hotel   5

Heat Genesis   6

On Ice   7

Snow Machines   10

Debt   11

Elegy with a Middle Seat   12

Three Versions   13

Arctic Negative   15

Arctic Current   16

ANWR   17

Morning Traffic   18

Here but Elsewhere   19

Territories   21

2.

Physical Retail   27

Poem with Ice and Breakup   28

Desire Swells   29

Here but Elsewhere   30

A Wave   32

Rhetorical Analysis   35

Play at Being People   36

The Basement   37

Lines toward Browerville, AK   38

Coast   39

Zen and the Organic   40

Evening Traffic   41

Set against White Background   42

Here but Elsewhere: Two Versions   43

3.

Last Sunset   47

Outside (of Life)   48

Still Storm   49

Here but Elsewhere   51

What Warmed   53

Landscape with Removal   54

Cemetery   55

Anthophobia   56

Tundra Forms   57

Winter Breaks   58

Summer Camp   59

Dancing in Atqasuk, AK   60

Here but Elsewhere   61

The Trouble   63

Acknowledgments   65

Of course spatiality and temporality are different from each other, but neither can be conceptualized as the absence of the other.

—Doreen Massey

Bedtime Story with Eagle and Sun

I'll tell you, once the darkness spread
hunger over our bodies, thirst into pores

dry for more than winter, after a thief
emptied tundra of its inner life, called it
Alaska, an eagle tried to find the sun

to find the sun drilled through the sky
to elsewhere, if you become night with me.

The eagle tracked the sun, that it bled
fugitive light. Our eyes waited as pebbles
washed over Utqiagvik Beach. After

years loud on land for its return, for ice
to break up, for melt to create kettle lakes

along tundra, we quieted. We didn't see
at first, the new of the old—we felt it
slicing caribou bellies, their warmth,

butchered and fueled by what had been
stolen from here, territories forced into

names, by stories we were made to read
in the voice of the page. It was fueled
with seal oil, whale fat, and each page

was sky for enough time the eagle wrote
light to fill all the absence in the arctic.

I.

Here but Elsewhere

Already sick, I waited for the doctor. Two
months later the appointment was canceled

as storm prevented flights into Atqasuk.
We build us alone. The solitary fox empties

the house of its many things. Days count
pills to pollute their bodies like ice warms

to its desires. Quiet deaths, these glaciers.
All the erratics, a kettle lake warms to boil.

———————

Sedge edges the village, spreads. *Dominant*

brings to mind curved landscapes—a city
against the foothills, ocean to shore—even

tundra where tussocks seek enough height

to flower. Even with that there are eyes
reaching. This landscape appears beyond

human shape. Even without that, names
mapped it, those eyes running horizons.

-40 degrees—to touch each other is arrival.

———

Thirty-third spring. Painted tundra fills
the time. It looks like a scene we might find

in the open room beyond this room, far past
ourselves—a parade of caribou eyes aimed.

Radiation Hotel

Part plastic guest
room. Part stunned body, skeletal

in the window, your mind—heat
funnels the body, ripples through.

Part of it too bruised
and empty around your stomach
to remove

the memory of your torso being dug
out, its impermanence
like a flower

bed—weeds and rodents threaten
to tell a story, begin overtaking.

Who is that story on its knees? That
part about the body

red as evening sky
above what you didn't believe.

What you didn't believe could
tunnel into you. That it already had.

Part climax. Part end.

Heat Genesis

The purged caribou heart. The first arctic
meal prepared raw before fire. Before fires

purpled meat, meat was ulued off to serve
an open mouth. The first heart's crevasses

stretched like caribou cut raw. Proto-heart
raw in search of fire, red windburn revealed

the body. That blood wanting of new heat
lived in the body raw. Open arctic, the first

blood transfusion was what caribou purged
fed into veins as freeze threatened the heart.

On Ice

1.

I've read ice referred to as earth's air conditioner. We sleep
as it forms, expands, melts—a simple process, as simple

as holding each other through night. The steps are exactly
the same for letting go of each other in the morning.

Swelling comes from being a world to yourself for too long.

2.

The skirring in the sky moves across the tundra. Across
Browerville's territory, shore is near white and fuels

what the rest of us feel—the ice rolls outward for maybe
the last few years that it will.

3.

At three my son palmed a burner red with heat. I pressed
ice against him and with freeze to his skin he knew

to go cold when hurting. He learned what to want for pain.
I'm going to jump in the lava, my son says. We are playing

in the backyard. He edges a hole our dog has emptied into
shape for years. Always the way it works, we remove

what makes us whole. He wants to be burned, he tells me,
and you can't save me. I act my own play-along scream

to the sky. He stops and says he will be okay. *Don't worry.
I promise it will be okay.* He jumps and I don't save him.

4.

Faces retain what the world gives back to us. We see it
in the mirror. Because it is already done, the mirror reflects

small ways we reduce. Like ice rolled over mistakes,
we grieve what we touch, the selves we try to change too late.

Sometimes we are awakened in time to know it. I once fell
through arctic ice hiding in a game of sardines. Broke

the surface and then almost drowned. I still miss the feeling
right after, the body's knowledge of almost dying but not.

5.

What I want is for my sons to survive long enough to see
what we each become, and to hold it until I break apart.

I want to write on ice. Enough to fall through it. Enough
to break the present moment backward. To numb

enough of the body to the point where I don't feel myself
holding me, that these arms might be someone else's arms

pulling me back up. Listen, most days we need to empty
the house of our ten thousand things. This harming warm

we splay for, these places we create, it all needs an ice bath
after the damage done here, needs a cry in cryotherapy.

6.

All the tears, translations we freeze for the future hurting.

Snow Machines

I never felt safe with one. So many accidents. So easy

to be obscure. So many winter nights, stranded hours
on the tundra. As they cross arctic territory on tracks

so much deflects against engine cowls, and the hiding
body. Easy to see 150 chemicals into air as metaphor

for what inside the North Slope is absent, so I don't.

Nights soaked in empty, we'd steal the ones left alone
and ditch them near the high school so they couldn't

be found. Once my friend Nathan drove his headfirst
into a pipe crossing the lagoon to Browerville—sober,

concussed, still alive, but nobody was heard saying so.

Debt

Your lips fitfully
give away the words.

Some of this currency
is voiced to others.

Some of this voice is
said back to yourself.

Elegy with a Middle Seat

After it all, a few friends and family, some poems
can never be more than the poems around them,
the entire crowd, a basket of words to ingest.
It is the same experiment with family members.
We have reasons Emily Dickinson never traveled
farther than she did. Or we think we do,
as we consider her personal life, her unseen parts
we describe with theories. We also have ways
of not traveling our distances. We have talks
about other people, the interior struggles
we loosely attribute to this or that thing we heard,
an oral history built communally. This terrifies me.
The armrest debate begins on the tarmac, extends
the sky's miles. I need to think about things.
I need to think about things outside this airplane.
I need the shadows of the pine trees at dusk
and what I have is shadows from the overhead
reading lights, thinking about Emily Dickinson
in the middle seat of a plane moving north,
two people squeezed around me, turbulence
touching us together in intervals. It raises
deathly images with these strangers and how not
touching takes more time to forgive than touching.
My friend Morgan wears superhero t-shirts.
My friend Spencer wears overalls and is sincere.
My friend Chris wears a confident leather jacket.
Something means more when you're less happy.
I consider the people seated next to me. I consider
whether or not they are my family for a few hours,
strangers positioning their shapes onto my own,
or if they are people paying to avoid themselves.

Three Versions

Sunday Brunch in NARL, AK, 1994

1.

Following thick, white lines of road, the outside
is smaller in winter, boundary to 100 mph
snowstorms. Hungry, we make it to the Naval
Arctic Research Laboratory (NARL), the glass
observatory that polar bears look into like a new
ocean, because that's what it is, a new world
for everyone thinking about survival, and food
from ingredients of words—*oil, salmon, eider,*
and *atmospheric sciences.* See the dark day?
It makes us cough, and then choke, this desire
like an enormous hunger we are taught to feed.

2.

Sundays we would eat all we could. Lines
of food up the coast from Barrow, in the name
of science. Where did all that food come from?
Midwinter and months since the barge
delivered our own grocery order. Twelve bucks
a person for this buffet, a deal when eggs
cost six dollars a dozen at Arctic Coast Trading
Post. I suppose we sat next to them, scientists
and researchers. It was all math and science
at NARL. Sometimes we waited for someone
to change the numbers, to find a new method
for explaining what it means to be alive here.

3.

If we are more than language. If what we are after
comes after something that we will never know
has its own truth for why caribou herds move
this way and not some other. If what we are after
is more than truth, more physical. If what we are
reflects in the ice more than houses on fire
during the duration between what is delivered
from the Beaufort Sea on barge and what is caught
by crew and rope, by what is given to the village
from water and what science delivers by order,
by receipt. Muktuk boils the way we boil, by time
and heat—more than truth, more than language.

Arctic Negative

Meade River, North Slope of Alaska

As we should always then remember to insist
that we shovel us over ourselves

after night-fire cooking what of the caribou
I vaguely remember what remains

is water lessening and hardening. Ptarmigan
hours, again. The salmonberry

days going unspoken away. Inupiaq if I can't
recover language outside the land.

The chum salmon and humpback whitefish

when I lack netting in the river. The lover
absent to whisper *this is all*

for us. Winter is standing up. To say that
nothing grows, it does—lichen

alive under snow, like thoughts. If this is all
for us, it is undone because of us.

I'm scrolling through all of myself in this
house of too many things. Current

pauses itself to reflect, then reverses stream.

Arctic Current

The youth I never had: cutting sockeye
up the belly, a tender line. We'd remove
the entrails. Then we'd cut off the head
to be returned into the water or buried
if we camped elsewhere. The backbone
pulled into air by our fingers, we'd hang
the body to dry from the rack of wood
made cross-like of fallen, retrieved sticks.

Beaches coasting Alaska, dots and lines
along an Arctic body, all I'd need is one
to become current for this moment now
that I'm ready to enter ice melt. I heard
if salmon become moldy, you form holes
three feet deep along the beach and soak
their bodies in salt water, pebbled shore
for the salmon, for the tide, for rebirth.

ANWR

1.

Given our sleep
into new

days, darkness
touches us,

melt waits
longer.

2.

There's no reason
to drill

ourselves
an emptiness
here and not feel

a body wanting
to hide.

Morning Traffic

Some caribou settle
in place with an early
hunger. You will hunt

what it is like you to
want, the slow desire

it eats. You can't hear
it first, but you will
run at the wide smell

of need. You will see
it is in your nature.

Here but Elsewhere

Absence is unresolved movement between two
events. At Meade River School we saw our home

outside the village. What forms in absence of sight

is body felt. We watched a body walk the unplowed
winter road parallel to our house but not reappear

to any eyes. My father ran home to catch the boy

using our phone. Ours was the only house he hoped
wouldn't question long-distance calls to a number

in Nome. After public safety listened, years after

the calls, he killed himself on his grandmother's
tundra grave. Presence is language the body learns.

I showed up at school every day to say the words
of others, voices keeping a record of my flattened

presence, its early static. Most winter days gathered
like absent bodies passed out from the below-zero

night, high in a bone-achy shack edging Browerville
where friends smoked out and then crashed, unsaid

skin unrecorded. Sitting quiet at a sanitized desk
voice-lacquered for certificates, I knew the absence

of veins in perfect attendance, the flatness of words inhaled to be spoken. The only answer was *here*.

Territories

Report paints grim picture about Alaska
Native language fluency, but hope remains

—KTUU, 2020

1.

I'm missing a language for what is lost.

Tundra. Tundra. Tundra. Tundra.
In difficulty, a grammar for the vastness

measured in millions of eye lengths.

I was raised without trees. In absence
and then out of nothing, Tundra.

I don't have a language that isn't white.

Or, like fog, if it is there it is set so
deep against white, I'm numb to its grip.

2.

Symptoms: all the colors of disease reflected.
Culture: white spreads the cold out.

Symptoms: sky replaced by deliveries.
Culture: every word for belief defined by sky.

3.

Accusation: every bowhead's death
                   expressed by the body.

Accusation: dark of winter, the home,
                   the body,
                            the abusive sun.

4.

The village voted itself dry
again. What is paradise

but a final tally of choices
given to innocence, sin

given to sunless days—
the caribou don't care

for laments. I do not see
any need between myself.

5.

Each cold
night

is code
to what

ripples
the body.

6.

Come February, draw two dots on the white
tundra. Move your head closer to both dots

until you can only see one of them. One

goes missing. That missing dot is everyone
from childhood, tundra littered with caribou.

2.

Physical Retail

Every stove is a complex system of human suffering.
How to sell your home: forget everything
you know about the violence of strangers and replace
that violence with upgraded appliances. Do we not
replace our hearts with other images? We do
our best to not replicate its beatings
when we see the face of someone arousing, the face
of someone who wants to tear our skin
from the body and wear it to dinner
only to say we are in a relationship,
the physical retail brought to you by desire.
Every stove is a trigger
to the past and in those moments we look around
the room for some stranger to pull it.
The violence with upgraded appliances
shimmers under the recessed lighting of a ceiling
pushing more toward the floor everyday. Do we
replicate the heart to eventually live without it?
The kitchen is quite warm this July, the weeks
where even wasps suffocate,
where every heart is a stove heating itself into flame.

Poem with Ice and Breakup

This season, you break apart to give space
to the version of yourself you no longer

map into your body, the shadow of self
Inupiat call *iḷitqusiq,* the spirit—three

letters between you and the word
for evil spirits, *iḷitqusiqḷuk*—detached—

three letters removed as you are removed
by someone from someone, the experience

seeing your ex-lover move farther away
from you, where you had both lived,

seeing this new couple that is not you—
you become unshelved in spring warmth,

aimless and unable to settle someplace, yet
you are cold and made colder. No language

explains why it works this way, a meaning
we lost over time or that never existed.

Desire Swells

The sea declares such a volume to body
shore, before you see whitecaps cresting

like a mouth as it breaks into you. You see
the edges of what it is
                                        to desire
                                                    desire,
a careful shade of eyes,
the curve of bone casting
                                        a shadow, swells
to embrace you and then
                                        embracing you

reach an inevitable and complete collapse
unseen in a privacy,
                        in such a brutal privacy.

Here but Elsewhere

1.

In Alaska, there are many degrees of thinking
your life is over, many ends to the body, like

the fall when I heard Eltron had returned
to Barrow, back from Anchorage and looking

for me. I never should have dated his girlfriend
those months he was in juvenile detention.

2.

Most searched: Mount McKinley's first ascent
                           is contagious.

Most searched: near Denali you have caught
                           something in the body.

3.

Proof: my son tells me he saw my father
last night as he slept. He doesn't know *dream*.

I show him a picture of my dad standing
on a fishing boat, Kodiak in the background—

his bearded face smiles back. *Yeah, that's him,*
your dad. And he knows you are my dad, too.

What did you guys talk about, I ask. *We didn't*
talk about anything, he says. *We just played.*

A Wave

The space of an event is that which opens up
by the gap that separates an effect from its causes.

—Slavoj Zizek

The lazy miracle a slipstream creates, we wake
out of the enormous night holding

flashlights to each other's eyes. We travel

the house's music, unseen life inside the silhouette
of our belongings, desire steeped in its own wild

division of things, the duffels full of clothes
in our closets, a drawer of lubrication to wet

the dangerous kisses. I can't recognize it all.
The tulips poison the house upon entering it.

I can't recognize the order of it all, the parties
responsible for such a disaster as poisoning

routines. I can't recognize it calling my name.

The night our house began to burn, the night
we might've never woken to the alarm in time,

we might have slept ourselves into the ground.
I can't imagine how to recognize holding

each other into a fire or what it might've saved,

the water needed to douse what electricity
started the flames. It's amazing how circuitry

can go wrong only to become exciting again
under different conditions, the alarm telling us

the story, as if we'd cut our ears off to avoid it,

our fears constructed in the grey smoke
between saving and being saved, or neither,

calling to us through the walls, not responding.
I remember running down the stairs together,

tripping over words in the haze, closely
related moments we hung on the walls,

habituated identities ghosted onto furniture,

particles in motion beyond themselves,
identifying a direction all together, all alone

when I witnessed the years we negotiated
in the unending days before the house's wiring

gave into itself. I can't recognize it's opposite,

the notion where divine grace enters the house
to deliver tulips and then torches the place.

Is it wrong to ask for salvation when the word
has no grounding in our home, no object

we attach to give image to our asking for it?
And why not say the words anyway

in whatever perverse manner we might conjure
a piano playing our way out of the flames?

An image comes to take us back in time.
It is desire. It is leftover food on the picnic table

as hail falls suddenly one June. It is our son's arm
caught underneath his body so he can't turn

in his crib where his torso shakes, broken
record-like, because he can't flip over at night.

It takes me
back to that place. It takes me back. It takes me.

Rhetorical Analysis

of the Arctic Ocean
completes a long

science. Tankers
declared oil majors
take their insides

after icepacks. No
trust in this cold

talking. Can fact
find its way
out of a mouth

that no longer
feels what it says?

Play at Being People

Where it rains, the potential to pour exists. When dogs eat grass farmers can predict that rain will come soon. Unscientific, yet this offers the opportunity to expect when things will get really shitty.

Late one morning, your car will get lifted by a helicopter and dropped in a nearby field, right onto some unsuspecting couple in love. The couple was only trying to have a picnic. Now they're smashed underneath your four-door sedan. And there is no going back. The police will identify your car then take you in for questioning and rough up your psyche a little. You have no defense. *A helicopter came and stole my car.* No one will ever believe in you. It doesn't help that you knew the couple, that you sent angry e-mails to one of them for a few months a few months ago. Those facts will mean everything when authorities can't find the helicopter you claim is responsible. Locals will be interviewed. One farmer will even say he saw something flying overhead that morning.

The Basement

How awful to say you miss someone. Months
and mouths are similar in that they close

year round. Clouds seem thicker. Gray appears
more gray. The black center of the cumulous

falls down from the weight of a collective mood.
It's the prevailing sentiment in the basement

where you sing to yourself. It doesn't need to be
a basement. If it were anyplace else,

clouds would be real. Sky would be real. Words
would be real. Even the body that's been missing

it, too, would come back to your waiting mouth,
your voice that until this point might not even exist.

Lines toward Browerville, AK

Living in absence is as inevitable
        as beach at high tide.

To signify what is taken, to say what is
        missing the turn home—

the emptiest of nights turns ceiling
        above the floor plan for absence.

Coast

No side of you in sight

at the parade, the flood
covers streets. It's all

one process. The ocean

grew a city. The city
then became an ocean

waves of bodies invade.
No life remains static.

Everything wedges you.

It overlaps in circles
the size of sky, shrouds

the body so precisely
you can't see, takes

a grainy picture you get

in the mail weeks later,
wherein you almost look

like one million other
faces look when seeing

one side of you, absent
any return address.

Zen and the Organic

I have never started a campfire
that didn't turn into a disaster

the size of Alaska, how flames
spread across my mind. I can't

name all the trees in my yard,
but I can talk my way up them.

Some drugs, the more you want
to unawaken into the sharp dark

a forest offers in the near winter.
I'll travel to the coastal range

to leave with a patch stitched

to my forehead. No place quiet
enough to take apart thoughts,

pills purify the un-seeable
bacteria in the water. Metaphor

for simile, down to the organic,
its stock photo, I look around

the dim earth to eventually see
one real apple blossom.

Evening Traffic

Some caribou take place with late hunger. If death is the mind
out of season, you hunt the sound of what it was

in the melt-filled space outside. You hear it beneath the lowest
tempo of need. You find it in your nature. Lost

on the trails of others, lost in reflection
most nights—memories like the melt that was once ice. What is

lost outside moves without you. The sound is one track playing
hours of your inside voice.

Set against White Background

Near the Arctic Coast Trading Post in Browerville,
searching for spring, not every thaw uncovers tracks.
Clotted Browerville buildings in blizzard, absence
reddens to what skin is there. The years since names
went missing from school days, they still elude scene.
Gone are gas, glue, and smoke into throats, chests,
for eventual hours this arctic would muddy streets
as the melt spreads like lies one June—no, every June.

Here but Elsewhere: Two Versions

I.

PERFORMANCE ON UTQIAGVIK BEACH

Circles of water   along the Beaufort Sea
Chukchi Sea   the aftermath   of equations

for survival   every ulu fails hands
frostbit
bruised   by ice cascading into itself

with as much as we can manage   to spare
                  of each other
the freeze coming off strangers   hitting

chests breathing yearly   breakups
of families   names left by the shore

to throw a pebble behind them   touched
by the body   to cast away   on the beach

what sickness follows   along the sand
to throw   it all behind   the body

as if those past tortures   inside and out
are events to keep   cleansed and clenched—

2.

SUNDAY BRUNCH IN NARL, AK

Stiff like tines
          pieces of human stuck
                    between teeth between

          silence between the silences
                    ingested

like *salmon*   *ptarmigan*
          eider and *lagoon*

all too much to see in the bright day

a past   where we are still flushed
with a great hunger   to touch one another—

3.

Last Sunset

Utqiagvik, AK, Early May

Darkness is animal. Hunting hours
nearby it attacks eyelids, rips apart

what weather holds, what it packs
to leave with it. You watch in need

of its contracting edges near a past
you once slept beside. The dark is

not darkness. It is you given leave
from the realness of seeing. Dark

in many things is only one thing
desire hides inside itself. There are

still beginnings that hurt, days you
claw your way back into your body.

Outside (of Life)

1.

Dark adaptation in December, tundra and the distant
remix of daylight—whatever it is that you are here

is broken, so you must survive your life—this skin
clinging so hard to itself against wind and clouds or fog—

2.

Once, Wanda Kippi's older brother, stuck in the storm
between Barrow and Atqasuk, spotted a caribou herd,

hunted one down, then slit its throat using a blade
from the broke-down snow machine, and drank its blood
to stay warm. After the storm, he walked to the village

with his wind-burned face beginning to peel back
dead layers, and some of the answers we were missing.

Still Storm

Utqiagvik mourns hunters killed as they towed whale home

—*Anchorage Daily News*, 2018

Because the water lost control, the crew delivered
what would temper—in the sea, in themselves—
the expectation of returning, because faces show
even in great bodies of water—that is, the Arctic's
declension—even nothingness strikes some faces
hard enough that we, too, look into our dressers
to find what has been mixed with all the receipts—
some folded letters, foreign money—so to avoid
grinding teeth into flecks, we release something
like prayer for the neighbor every morning, his
tools delivered to some site, because it is not
our body punished by the machine as it steers
the days, these hourly vessels of life, but instead
the other shadows inside waves before waves
release into stillness, forgetting what it is they were
called for, that they were taking the men, men
raised together into a body of water called family
to mean more than simply *crew,* because a crew
suggests military force, the imposed expeditions
into so many other types of deaths, not these men
from childhood, men who, even if we hate
what has now become of ourselves, sick enough
for our bodies to end as anything but themselves,
brought the bowhead home as they promised to it
they would, even in the building weather, men
who won't walk the village again, which is why

no one wanted to talk to the reporter, declining
to release anything, because *release,* in legal terms,
means to give to others what rightfully chose you.

Here but Elsewhere

The absence is enormous in the Arctic.

Christian's mother died when a rope
broke as she helped pull the bowhead

onto the beach, its recoil force enough

to kill what it hit the moment it did.
Some deaths create other ways to die.

Some losses you only understand once

your body and mind come back together
wherever it is beyond what we name.

———————

On this street or that one, on Fireweed
or Tudor, maybe downtown Anchorage,

their blocks on my breath, if I see a story
repeat a gesture and fall, maybe like Jonah

would have years ago, winter on his face,
will it return as pores release in the night?

As we tilted our cold necks to the floor

one friend stood behind and pushed
hard on the back of our heads to make us

black out. We tried to turn off, inhaling

days with every drug hidden in school
to leave ourselves and return metaphors.

What Warmed

Not Atqasuk's raw edges reduced into kettle
lakes. Not raised buildings, iced sewage under.
It wasn't our mukluks hanging outside, the furs
shaped over trails of arctic desire, acres and acres
of it, and all that swelling inside us. Not trigger
and bullet waiting for muscle contractions. Not
muktuk, the ocean currents. What tried to retake
soil, what drilled down, what burrowed into sedges,
nested owl mounds, the lemmings dead after melt.

Landscape with Removal

Boundaries are disorder. It's not real to find a future absent loss.
In one spring, a borough crew dismantled aboveground utilidors
that carried our water and sewage from Browerville apartments.

Buildings are disorder. One March before the utilidors were torn
apart, my father died in Atqasuk's gymnasium. Arterial, the arctic
crisscrossing of rivers and other melt. The new ice road they made

shapes order from Browerville to Atqasuk. It might take me back
there to settle things, to have some direction for what unattached.
Beliefs are disorder. What possesses wind is night-like thinking.

Cemetery

Flowers like credit
card offers.

Petals pulled away
like eyelids

from bulbs.
I can't even watch
          your plot.

Anthophobia

Because the car drives too fast into nothing
        but horizon and other cars

look like flowers out of focus, broken alive
        in fields. Because it's dark to believe

how a bed oscillates between comfort
        and suffocation by sheets. Because

flowers replace gravesites like candles replace
        light the body needs. Because smells

live deeper than touch. Because water washes
        even determined insects from petals

and people, and people never make the world
        more than machine, even if they want

blood. Because the threat is often more a smell.
        Because all things die by stem.

Tundra Forms

I receive experience quietly, like tundra
        disappears stories. Below lupine
            and willow

                  permafrost
is conjunction.

The frost covering the windows is called
fern frost or *ice flowers.*

        As if I had to recover, it is called
            winter. As if I am
the artificial

room, I give in to the desire
        to hurt flowers with my hand—

into pieces
as if my fingers were the teeth
of a saw. It is called *field dressing* because

                I am taken apart
like an animal on the tundra.

Winter Breaks

all evening into the house—
distortions of tundra

as sky undresses ice, snow
drifts against the mind

until the ice is unseeable
night, open in spots.

Summer Camp

After the bull caribou falls, the herd dissolves momentarily, dust pulled
into air—then a glassy silence, but mostly a slight, unpretending breeze.

Shed of their velvet, his antlers are a full red. Imagine warm
blood setting. What is taken apart   is also reduced to more—

heart and liver like lessening fires
tamped from flame   by the crystal-white outline closing in.

Dancing in Atqasuk, AK

Evenly distanced and stomping as a herd
        of drilling wells, every arm cuts

in directions not unlike water. Drums
        to beat into, their time is absorbed

like the cloudberries called salmonberries
        called aqpiks in the late summer

of our hands. Under feet, needles
        leave the room for a time difference.

Here but Elsewhere

Language doesn't make decisions. It keeps
guessing. When I was given my Inupiaq

name, Jenny Felder talked me into sounds

from the book listing each possible version
nearby. I still hear her. I would speak them

now if my mouth could shape the words.

———————

Snow takes the most of us when it comes
to fall. In what felt like Spokane's worst

snowstorm for decades, my brother and I
only had mukluks for our feet, the fur warm

and foreign, absent of what had sold out
in stores across the white city. All we had

was distance. All we wanted, the snow
boots with the Velcro every other kid wore.

———————

We carry too much of the past. Expansive
bodies like snow melt. It's not the only thing

leaving, leaving, leaving. It melts into smaller

bodies of water, so we must wade through it
to the source, because the arctic doesn't freeze

itself. It grows into what it must be, and is.

The Trouble

1.

Memory creates impossible versions.

2.

The old stories: a clay lover
cannot cross water. A lover made of iron
cannot move through a furnace.

A wooden lover cannot pass through fire
to run back from the wild and find us.
We cannot build a life with desire.

3.

We don't write the enviable into life.
We don't awaken a fire from sleep.

There are promises and wishes
no one makes simultaneously.

4.

If we could butcher desire into parts,
the things we could have built here.

ACKNOWLEDGMENTS

Many thanks to the editors, readers, and staff at the following publications where some of my work appeared, sometimes in different forms. There were so many instances where their feedback and ideas helped bring these poems along:

Adroit: "A Wave"; *Arts & Letters*: "Desire Swells" & "The Trouble"; *Atlanta Review*: "Tundra Forms" & "Arctic Negative"; *Cider Press Review*: "Cemetery" & "Anthophobia"; *Conjunctions* (online feature): "Heat Genesis"; *decomp*: "Debt"; *Dogwood*: "Here but Elsewhere: Two Versions"; *Florida Review*: "Still Storm," "Bedtime Story with Eagle and Sun," "On Ice," & "Snow Machines"; *ILK*: "Play at Being People"; *Laurel Review*: "Territories" & "Here but Elsewhere"; *Michigan Quarterly Review*: "Here but Elsewhere" series of poems; *Mississippi Review*: "Radiation Hotel"; *Moon City Review*: "Last Sunset" & "Summer Camp"; *Pacifica Literary Review*: "Morning Traffic"; *Poetry Daily*: "Here but Elsewhere" ("Already sick . . ." & "The absence is enormous . . ."); *Sonora Review*: "Outside (of Life)"; *Southern Review*: "Poem with Ice and Breakup" & "Three Versions"; *Tupelo Quarterly*: "The Basement"; *Western Humanities Review*: "Physical Retail" & "Coast," "Zen and the Organic," & "Elegy with a Middle Seat"; *Worcester Review*: "Dancing in Atqasuk, AK."

I'm grateful to the editors at *Poetry Daily* for reprinting part of "Here but Elsewhere."

Part of the "Here but Elsewhere" series was awarded the Goldstein Poetry Prize from the *Michigan Quarterly Review*, selected by final judge A. Van Jordan.

"Bedtime Story with Eagle and Sun," "On Ice," & "Snow Machines" were named finalists for the Editor's Prize and published by the *Florida Review*.

"Radiation Hotel" was selected as a finalist for the *Mississippi Review* Poetry Prize.

Some of these poems appeared in a chapbook called *The Territorial*, winner of the *Laurel Review*'s Midwest Chapbook Prize and published by GreenTower Press. Thanks to the amazing team at the *Laurel Review* for their work on the chapbook.

My love and thanks to Rebecca Shepard.

To Linda Shepard and Derek Shepard, for influence and care.

To all my family and friends—they are in and between the lines of these poems.